THE
STAFFORDSHIRE
MOORLANDS

Volume 1

A Portrait in Photographs and Old Picture Postcards

by

W. George Short

S. B. Publications
1991

First published in 1988 by Brampton Publications.

This edition published October 1991 by S. B. Publications,
Unit 2, The Old Station Yard, Pipe Gate, Market Drayton, Shropshire, TF9 4HY.

© Copyright S. B. Publications 1991.

All rights reserved.

ISBN 1 85770 002 3

Printed in Great Britain by Rubell Print Ltd., Bunbury, Tarporley, Cheshire, CW6 9PQ.

Bound by J. W. Braithwaite and Son Limited, Pountney Street, Wolverhampton WV2 4HY.

CONTENTS

	Page
Introduction	
Acknowledgements	
BLYTHE BRIDGE	1 – 4
CAVERSWALL	5 – 11
DILHORNE	12 – 15
FORSBROOK	16 – 19
DRAYCOTT	20 – 21
CRESSWELL	22
TOTMONSLOW	23
CHECKLEY	24 – 26
TEAN	27 – 43
HUNTLEY	44
FREEHAY	45 – 47
THREAPWOOD	48

CONTENTS CONTINUED

	Page
CHEADLE	49 – 65
KINGSLEY HOLT	66 – 68
KINGSLEY	69 – 77
WERRINGTON	78
FROGHALL	79 – 80
THE WOODHOUSE	81
HAWKSMOOR	82 – 83
OAKAMOOR	84 – 99
COTTON	100 – 103
ALTON CASTLE	104 – 106
ALTON VILLAGE	107 – 113
ALTON LODGE / ABBEY / TOWERS	114 – 119
DIMMINGSDALE LODGE	120

INTRODUCTION

The district of the Staffordshire Moorlands was formed as a result of the 1974 Local Government Act, whereby the former District Council of Cheadle and Leek and Biddulph Urban Council were merged to form the new Staffordshire Moorlands District Council.

When planning a nostalgic book about the Staffordshire Moorlands, it was soon discovered that it would be impossible to feature everything in one book. Therefore, this first volume illustrates the towns, villages and area, south of the A52.

The nostalgic tour commences in Blythe Bridge, then, Caverswall, Dilhorne — at one time the residence of the Lord of the Manor of Cheadle, Draycott, Cresswell where the Catholic faith was maintained through the years of repression, and on to the district boundary at Checkley where there is a fine 12th century church (Grade One listed).

The tour returns to Tean where the tape industry flourished for over 200 years, and on to the market town of Cheadle, entered in the Domesday Book, as was Kingsley which at one time was a Royal Manor and of late has had an industrial community.

To conclude, the tour visits Oakamoor, where for many generations copper and brass manufacture took place, Cotton, and finally, Alton and Alton Towers — the ancestral home of the Earls of Shrewsbury.

I trust that this book will evoke many happy memories and give as much pleasure as I have had in selecting the photographs and postcards.

W. George Short
Cheadle
August, 1988

In the same series: The Staffordshire Moorlands Volume 2.

ACKNOWLEDGEMENTS

To the photographers of yesteryear whose views are now recorded in this book for posterity.

I am grateful to Brampton Publications for their kind invitation to compile this collection of photographs and postcards of the area, and I am indebted to the many people and various organisations who have given me information, or who have allowed me to inspect their records, in particular:—

Mr. D. V. Fowkes, B.A., M.A., F.S.A., County Archivist
The Trustees of the William Salt Library
The staff at the County Record Office, Stafford.
Mrs. J. Hampartumain, Assistant Archivist, Lichfield Record Office
Public Record Office, Kew
The National Society (C. of E.) for Promoting Religious Education, London
M. B. S. Exham, Esq., Diocesan Registrar, Lichfield
Rev. P. Dennison, Roman Catholic Diocesan Archivist, Birmingham
Blagg, Son and Masefield, Solicitors of Cheadle
Mrs. M. Philips, Heath House, Tean
Mr. A. Hollingsworth, Alton Towers PLC
My son, Ian, for script reading
Mrs. G. Jackson for editorial
Steve Benz for additional editorial and marketing

THE RAILWAY STATION, BLYTHE BRIDGE, c. 1950
Built by the North Staffordshire Railway Company, the station opened on 7th August, 1848.
Its first Station Master was Mr. William Vyse.
The crossing gates, seen in the distance, were replaced by a barrier erected between
the 2nd and 16th March, 1980, at which time the signal box was also demolished.

THE SMITHFIELD HOTEL, BLYTHE BRIDGE, c. 1912
In 1921, the then proprietor, Mr. Arthur Keeling, commenced a local 'bus service named "Old Bill" which operated from the stables behind the Hotel.
The service ran from Cheadle to Longton until it was closed in 1932.
On the right is the Cattle Market auction room.

CHEADLE ROAD, BLYTHE BRIDGE, c. 1920
On the left is the wall around the grounds of Blythe House.
On the right is Church Terrace.
In 1913, the Telephone Exchange moved from Rose Cottage (by the railway station) to No. 10, Church Terrace, where it remained until 1940 when the Exchange went automatic. The last hand-operator was Mrs. Davies.

BLYTHE HOUSE, 1910

Erected in 1879, this was the family home of Charles Harvey and, later, of T. C. Wild. It was occupied until 1927, when it was vacated, subsequently to be demolished in the 1930's. Previously, on this site, there stood a local Charity Trust School, built in 1728, under the Will of William Amery and endowed with over seven acres of land called Pool Street Meadows, value £37. The Trust is still in being and is available for the benefit of the four schools and scholars in the Parish of Blythe Bridge and Forsbrook.

CAVERSWALL CHURCH.

ST. PETER'S CHURCH, CAVERSWALL, c. 1910
Originally consecrated in 1230, the Church was rebuilt in 1663, when the Sanctuary
was raised by 3 feet.
The door and hinges bear a date of 1667.
The Church is a "weeping church" — that is, it leans to one side — in this case the right.

ST. PETER'S CHURCH, CAVERSWALL, c. 1920
On the right, the pulpit is the original one, from the days of box pews.
The Communion Table, dated 1633, has St. Peter and shell designs indicating fishermen.
On the left side there is the Countess St. Vincent memorial, made by Chantrey in 1818.
The organ was built by Oakes of Meir Heath and is the 1914-18 War Memorial.
Electricity was installed in the Church in August 1938 by Morris & Co. of Burslem,
at a cost of £67.

CAVERSWALL SQUARE, c. 1906
The "Town Hall" mentioned in the postcard title is the Tree in the centre of the Square. The one in the picture is the old Constable Wick tree which was planted here in 1672. This was replaced by a new tree planted by Caverswall Parish Council on 9th March, 1935. The building on the right is The Red House public house, whose first entry in directories is dated 1834, when William Bradbury was the brewer.

THE NATIONAL SCHOOL, CAVERSWALL, c. 1902

A school was first built on this site in July 1824, costing £300, of which the National Society gave a grant of £100. In 1861, the School was rebuilt and enlarged at a cost of £758. On 1st May, 1903 the School was taken over by the Local Education Authority Board and has subsequently been extended by the County Council and Church Authorities in 1956, 1974 and 1985.

Roman Catholic Church & Castle Lodge, Caverswall.

ROMAN CATHOLIC CHURCH AND CASTLE LODGE, CAVERSWALL, c. 1905
The Roman Catholic Church is dedicated to St. Filumena and was opened by Bishop Ullathorne on Thursday, 28th January, 1864. It cost £1700 to build, the gift of J. P. P. Radcliffe, Esq. of Caverswall Castle. The architect was Mr. Gilbert Blount of London and the builder was Mr. Lewis Jefferies of Stone. Mr. Radcliffe also funded the erection of the Presbytery and the Roman Catholic School, at this time. To the right of the Church (in the picture) is the West Lodge of the Castle, built by Mr. W. E. and Mrs. A. Bowers in 1890.

CAVERSWALL CASTLE, 1858
(from a drawing by Harriet Blagg)
Church records state that a castle was built with a moat and three drawbridges in 1322 but the present castellated mansion house was built by Matthew Cradock in 1625.
A chapel in the Castle was registered at the Easter Sessions in 1813.

CAVERSWALL CASTLE
This photograph of the oak panelled hallway was taken at a time when the nuns of the Order of the Daughters of the Heart of St. Mary were in residence.
The Castle was a religious community building from 1811 to 1840 and then from 1933 to 1977.
It is now a private residence.

DILHORNE CHURCH AND OLD GRAMMAR SCHOOL

A school was founded by the Earl of Huntingdon in the reign of Henry VIII and the School building shown was erected by the Marquis of Hastings in 1837. It was in use as a boys' Church School until 1876 when the present School was built for both boys and girls. The first masters for the new School were Mr. and Mrs. Hutchinson.

Children of Dilhorne may still receive benefits from the sixteenth century Endowment of this School. (Photograph reproduced by permission of the Trustees of the William Salt Library, Stafford).

ALL SAINTS CHURCH, DILHORNE, c. 1920
The rare octagonal tower, containing six bells, is part of the original Church, dedicated in 1166.
The Nave and aisles were rebuilt in 1819 at a cost of £1,000.
Inside the Church there are memorials to the Manningham-Buller family, Lords of the Manor of Dilhorne.
The memorial in the foreground is to the Slater family.

DILHORNE HALL
The first Hall to stand on this site was erected in 1270 and this was replaced in 1377 by a second Hall. The picture shows the third Hall which was built in 1837 to the design of Trubshaw of Great Haywood, for Edward Buller.
The Hall was vacated by the family in 1924 and put up for sale in 1927.
It was subsequently demolished and the stone used for road making.
The Crown Bowling Green of Dilhorne Recreation Centre is now on the site of the Hall.

HIGH STREET, DILHORNE, 1910
The village street is seen here with, on the left, the Post Office, where members of
the Dale family were Postmasters for over eighty years.
The building on the right was originally the Tollgate House, built in 1762.
Later, it became the Police Station house and is now a private residence.

TOLLGATE HOUSE, FORSBROOK
The house was erected in 1838 at a cost of £134.10s.0d. and
stood at the corner of Dilhorne Road and Cheadle Road.
It closed as a toll house in 1878 and was sold as a private residence.
It was demolished in the 1960's.

CHEADLE RD, FORSBROOK.

CHEADLE ROAD, FORSBROOK, c. 1920
On the right is "The Bulls Head" public house and lower down, "The Butchers Arms".
Beyond, but not in the picture, is "The Roebuck Inn".
Three public houses without a house between!
Further up this road, on the left-hand side, there stood another public house,
"The Miners Arms".

FORSBROOK SQUARE, c. 1910

Until 1905, a small cottage stood in the middle of the Square.
The building on the left was the Grimwade Memorial Hall, built and opened in 1906, in memory of Minnie Eileen Grimwade. The Hall was used for temperance meetings and Methodist Sunday Schools were held upstairs.
The Hall was demolished in 1927.

ST. PETER'S CHURCH, FORSBROOK, 1910
Designed by Mr. Barr of London, the Church was built by Mr. Goldstraw of Wetley Rocks
at a cost of £1,100. The corner stone was laid by Rev. E. Whieldon, Rural Dean, on
7th June, 1847 and the Church was consecrated by the Bishop of the Diocese on
11th January, 1849.
At the Consecration Service the collection taken amounted to £87.1s.6d.
The East Window was installed in memory of Charles Harvey.

ST. MARGARET'S CHURCH, DRAYCOTT IN THE MOORS, c. 1915
The Church was first built and consecrated in 1268, rebuilt in 1727 and restored in 1848, with the clock being installed in 1889.
The tower holds eight bells, the dates of which range from 1604 to 1939.
The Communion Table was given to the Church by the people of Oakamoor in October, 1967.

ST. MARGARET'S CHURCH, DRAYCOTT IN THE MOORS
This is the Draycott Chapel where the Draycott family tombs are preserved.
The oldest tomb is that of Sir Richard Hugo de Dracot whose effigy,
in ringed chain-mail, dates from 1255-65 A.D.
At the rear of the Church is housed an oak chest bearing a date of 1270.
It was transferred from Rookery Farm in 1846, after being bricked up in a
chimney recess from the time of Cromwell.

ST. MARY'S ROMAN CATHOLIC CHURCH, CRESSWELL, 1933

In 1791 it became legal for Catholics to own places of worship and in 1816 Father Baddeley, Parish Priest, set about building the present Church. Prior to this time the local Roman Catholics had held their services in a chapel in Paynsley Hall.

Lady Mary Stourton, a member of the family who owned the Draycott estates, provided the necessary funds of £800 to build the Church.

Cresswell is the Mother Church of the northern part of the Diocese. The other churches are at Alton, Caverswall, Cheadle, Cobridge, Leek, Longton and Newcastle-under-Lyme.

TOTMONSLOW, TEAN HALT, c. 1920
The railway line from Cresswell to Totmonslow and on to Cheadle was authorised on 24th May, 1887.
The first stage was cut in 1888 and the line between Cresswell and Totmonslow was opened on 7th November, 1892 with the continuation to Cheadle being opened on 1st January, 1901.
The whole line was closed to passenger traffic on 17th June, 1963.

CHURCH LANE, CHECKLEY, c. 1920
The lane leads to Deadmans Green and the first Ebenezer Chapel, erected in 1821. It was also the main thoroughfare prior to the turnpike road being cut in c. 1780. In 1913, behind the trees on the left-hand side, Mrs. Hurst opened Checkley's first Post Office — where it still remains to this day.

ST. MARY'S AND ALL SAINTS CHURCH, CHECKLEY, 1841
(from a drawing by J. Buckler)

The Church was consecrated in 1196 and the right of Patronage was held by the Beke family. The Patronage was sold in 1589, again in 1805 and, later, was purchased by the Philips family who still own it. The drawing shows, on the left, behind the Nave buttress, a small single storey building. This was erected in 1839 and used first as a Sunday School and then, in 1874, it opened as Checkley National Day School with Miss Emma Shaw, the mistress. It remained a school until the new school was built in 1879, when this building was taken down and re-erected as the reading room in Lower Tean.
(Drawing reproduced by permission of the Trustees of the William Salt Library, Stafford).

**ST. MARY'S AND
ALL SAINTS CHURCH,
CHECKLEY,** c. 1908
The fine East Window and chancel
windows depict the crests
of many notable local families.
According to records,
the chancel stalls were given by
Anthony Draycott in 1550.
The organ, on the left, was given by
the Vernon family as a
Thanksgiving gift on their fiftieth
Wedding Anniversary in 1906.
In 1916, the Altar in the
photograph was given to the
Chapel in the North
Staffordshire Royal Infirmary
and replaced by a new
High Altar, riddel posts and
hanging frontals.
Designed by J. N. Comper,
they were installed in memory
of John W. Philips and dedicated
by Lord Bishop Kempthorne
on 4th April, 1916.
In the foreground there is a
Saxon Baptismal Font.
Electricity, installed by
C. A. Newton & Co. of Derby,
at a cost of £103, replaced the
oil lamps in 1935.

THE HEYBRIDGE, LOWER TEAN, c. 1931
From its purchase in 1813 to being vacated in 1945,
this was the home of one of the branches of the Philips family.
The house was later demolished.

HIGH STREET, TEAN, c. 1905
This view is looking east with, on the left, the Black's Head Hotel, first recorded in the directories of 1818. On the right, the four storey building is part of Philips' Tape Mill, erected in 1881. Beyond is the three storey mill erected by Trubshaw in 1822. In this mill was a Boulton Watt steam engine — used to provide power for operation of the tape looms. Among the rules for employment, in the early days, were punishments by fine. Fines imposed: 1d. if you swore; 1d. if you closed a window.

28

HIGH STREET, TEAN, c. 1929
On the left is Steele's, the Post Office, the Title Deeds of which date from 22nd December, 1866.
Next to it is a private dwelling house and bay-windowed shop.
Beyond, is a large three storey brick building with a porch over the door and the Title Deeds of this house date from 16th June, 1876. The building was let as a Temperance and Reading Room.
In the Philip's Estate sales of 1916 and 1942, many of the terraced houses in Tean were sold to sitting tenants for between £80 and £100 each. The Post Office was listed as Lot 17 in the sale brochure of 1916.

HIGH STREET, TEAN, c. 1897
This view, looking west, shows the decorations for the Diamond Jubilee Celebration of Queen Victoria. On the left is the J. & N. Philips' Tape Mill.
An extract from work books details the cost of work done on the Mill:
December 1821, "to build chimney, two workmen — 9 days and Samuel Barlow — 8 days = 16 shillings, Liquer when finished chimney — 15 shillings; liquer for Ingin man — 4 shillings."
The archway in the Mill was built by Trubshaw's men in January 1822 using 1,920 arch bricks, costing 8/-.
In the right foreground is the Temperance and Reading Room.

J. & N. PHILIPS' TAPE MILL, TEAN
The photograph shows a weaver, Mr. Jack Allen, operating one of the early tape looms. On the right, on an iron frame can be seen the initials N P — Nathanial Philips. The Indentures of 1750/51 show a person "shall be instructed in the mystery or business of tape weaving and shall not reveal to anyone, the art or mystery of weaving. The instruction period shall be from eleven months to eleven months until seven times eleven months have expired and for three months after." Note the single lamp over the loom. Prior to installation of gas or electricity, illumination was by candle — one per loom.

HIGH STREET, TEAN, c. 1907
Looking westwards down High Street and showing a butcher's shop on the left.
In the right foreground is the blacksmith's shop and a gas lamp
is fixed to the wall of the adjacent building.
The road is made of earth and hard core.

CHRIST'S CHURCH, TEAN

20th June, 1842

This is the cover of the invitation to attend the laying of the Foundation Stone of the "new Church" in 1842.
The architect and builder was Johnson, son-in-law of Trubshaw of Great Haywood.
Rev. C. B. Charlewood, who laid the stone, resided at Oakhill, Tean.
The Treasurer was Mr. J. Wood, manager of Tean Hall Mill and the churchwardens were Mr. Thomas Weston and Mr. Henry Mountford.
Rev. William Hutchinson was rector of Checkley, at the time, and the curate was Rev. W. Higton, who was later to be the first vicar of Tean.

THE CEREMONY OF
LAYING THE FOUNDATION STONE
OF THE
NEW CHURCH,
TO BE CALLED CHRIST'S CHURCH,
AT UPPER TEAN, IN THE PARISH OF CHECKLEY,

WILL (WITH DIVINE PERMISSION) TAKE PLACE

ON MONDAY, THE 20th OF JUNE, 1842.

The Procession will commence at One o'clock.

ORDER OF PROCESSION.

FROM THE BRIDGE AT TEAN, TO THE SITE OF THE NEW CHURCH.

Miss Lowe's Infant School Children.
Mrs. Wood, Girls School, Mrs. Gimbert.
Mr. Sinzininex, Tean School Boys.
Mr. William Arnold, Checkley Church Sunday Scholars.
Architect.   Builder.
Treasurer.
Churchwardens.
The Rev. C. B. Charlewood, who is to lay the Foundation Stone.
The Rector.   The Curate.
Rural Deans.
Clergy of the Neighbourhood.
Subscribers and Parishioners.

The Clergy are requested to attend in their Gowns.

Subscriptions will be received by Mr. Wood, of Tean Hall; The Rev. W. Hutchinson, Checkley; or the Rev. W. Higton, Tean.

CHRIST'S CHURCH, TEAN, c. 1920
The cost of building the Church, using Hollington stone, was £1,575.
The Church was consecrated on 10th July, 1843 by the Bishop of Hereford,
the Rt. Rev. Thomas Musgrove. The Archdeacon of Stoke, George Hodson,
preached the sermon and the collection at the service was £50.
Tean became an ecclesiastical parish on 20th August, 1844.
The present incumbent is eleventh in succession at Tean.

HEATH HOUSE, TEAN, 1824
(from a drawing by Sarah Pease dated 1824)
This House, built in 1690, was vacated on 21st December, 1835
and pulled down in May, 1836.
Eight of the columns shown were taken down and erected in the wood nearby.
This is now known as The Templewood.
(Photograph reproduced by permission of Mrs. M. Philips).

HEATH HOUSE, TEAN, c. 1920

Built and designed by Thomas Johnson, the Foundation Stone was laid on 2nd July, 1836. John Burton Philips and his wife, Joanne, moved into their new home on 15th June, 1840. During World War II the House was taken over as a Red Cross Hospital.
Heath House is the only House in the area built by a family and still retained and lived in by a successive member of that family.
(Photograph reproduced by permission of Mrs. M. Philips).

TEAN BRITISH SCHOOL, c. 1910

The Preliminary Statement on Education in Tean in 1846 stated that a new school is to be built and "a preference is given to the children of parents in the employ of J. & N. Philips & Co., but no child is refused admittance if there is room for them".

Built by Thomas Johnson for J. & N. Philips & Co., the Deeds are dated 16th June, 1854. From inception a member of the Philips family has been on the Governors Board. The log book commences on 20th April, 1863. The School was leased by J. & N. Philips & Co. to the Staffordshire County Council Education Authority from 25th December, 1929, when it became an official Council School. On 25th April, 1939, the company sold the school and site to Staffordshire County Council and it is now known as Greatwood Primary School.

ROMAN CATHOLIC CHURCH AND SCHOOL, TEAN, c. 1930
The centre part of the above building was erected in 1837 as a Primitive Methodist Chapel.
It opened on 10th September, 1837 and, after some forty years, the Chapel closed.
The building was reopened as a Roman Catholic School on 7th October, 1889 and the site and
School were purchased by the Catholic authorities in 1894, for £194.
The room to the left was subsequently added and it was then used as a Church and School until the new
Church, St. Thomas', was built and opened on 13th July, 1938. The new School opened in January, 1969.

CORNER OF BACK LANE AND NEW ROAD, TEAN, 1907
The photograph shows members of the Wesleyan Church being conveyed by wagonette to the Woodhead Hall Sunday School Anniversary.
The building behind the horse's ears is the School House. Records state that "the building was erected by J. & N. Philips in 1810 for a Sunday School and Chapel, but was not used as a Chapel after 1819". It was used as a daily and Sunday School and was replaced in 1854 when the Tean British School was built.

WESLEYAN METHODIST CHAPEL, TEAN

The first Wesleyan Chapel in Tean was built in 1821 and adjoined the end terrace house in Uttoxeter Road, (since demolished).
The above Chapel was built during 1843 and cost £630.1s.10d.
It opened on 21st December, 1843.
The last service in the Chapel was conducted on Sunday 29th December, 1985 by Rev. D. Watson, assisted by Rev. R. W. Hubball and Rev. C. E. Collin.
The Chapel was demolished during the first week of February 1988.

TEAN HOME GUARD, 1940-45
During World War II the Home Guard met in the Village Hall, under the command of Captain Reg Stagg. His Lieutenants were Arthur Chadwick and Frank Salt. They had duty rosters for night duties and were on guard at Heath House tower and other high points. Rifle training was held at Newton Farm.

DOUBLE ROW, CHEADLE ROAD, TEAN, c. 1952

These eight houses were built by J. & N. Philips & Co. in 1798, for their weavers, at a cost of £1,467. On the ground floor were the looms which were operated by hand and measured 6ft. 2in. to 8ft. 3in. long. The frames of wood were 4 inches thick and their height was 8 feet. The weaver's family accommodation was upstairs and there was an attic in the roof for storage. In 1822, when the mills were built, the looms were called into the mill and the houses were converted to wholly family accommodation. The houses were demolished in June 1966 and Senior Citizens' bungalows now stand on the site.

THE CROFT, TENFORD, c. 1950

This terrace of eight houses was erected by J. & N. Philips in 1829. They were artisan dwellings for the dyers and crofters who were employed at the mills of Cheadle and Tean. Behind the houses are the old croft buildings which have dates of 1829 on the archway leading to the bleach house and 1841 on the drying house.
Fields and gardens were rented out to Philips & Co. for use as drying areas, with rents varying from 3/- to 6/9d. per year.

HUNTLEY HALL, HUNTLEY, c. 1921

The Hall was built in the 1820's for Captain Clement Sneyd, R.N. who, from 1837 to 1840 was Churchwarden at Cheadle Parish Church. He was promoted to Rear Admiral in 1846 and died in 1851. On his death, the Hall passed to his daughter who married George Mather, the first Parish Priest at St. Chad's, Freehay.
The centre part of the Hall was demolished in 1929.

ST. CHAD'S CHURCH, FREEHAY, c. 1920
The Church was built between September 1842 and December 1843, when it was opened by License, to be consecrated on 22nd December, 1846.
The architect was G. Gilbert Scott, the builder was Evans of Ellastone and it was furnished with Minton tiles.
The Foundation Stone, laid by Captain Sneyd of Huntley Hall, is under the centre east window light.

ST. CHAD'S CHURCH, FREEHAY, c. 1920
The first sermon was preached on the morning of Sunday, 10th December, 1843, the text being taken from the Book of Acts. On either side of the Altar, on the floor, are memorial brass plates to Rev. George Mather, the first vicar, and to Rev., later Bishop, Richard Rawle, founder of the Church. On 25th April, 1935, Rev. W. H. Greening, Vicar of Freehay, wrote to the Rector of Cheadle requesting the old Communion rails of Cheadle Church; the rails were transferred to Freehay later that year — where they remain to this day.
The three lights of the tall East Windows are by William Wailes, the gift of the Rev. G. Grote.

FREEHAY NATIONAL SCHOOL, c. 1930
In July 1845, records show that a school was held in two cottages maintained by the vicar, Rev. G. Mather. In 1846 an application was made to erect a purpose-built school. The new school, containing three classrooms, and the adjoining teacher's house were built at a total cost of £750 made up as follows: £700 for the building, £30 for the land, £10 for the fittings and £10 for the conveyance.
The School log books open on 1st October, 1863, with James Bell and Frances Chawner as certified teachers and Mary Pollard, the pupil teacher. The log books close on 4th August, 1981 stating "School opened for the last time today". In 1987 the School was sold as a private residence.

"GREEN MAN" INN.
(Lot 27.)

THE GREEN MAN, THREAPWOOD, 1913
This licensed house was Lot 27 and sold for £875 in the sale of the Earl of Macclesfield's Estate on Thursday 17th July, 1913.
Included with the sale were farm buildings and 37 acres, 16 perches of farmland.
The licensed house had a six day license.
It was converted into the Highwayman Inn in the 1960's.

PLANTATION HOUSE, CHEADLE, 1922

Built in 1855 for the family of Thomas MacKenzie, it was constructed by William Alcock of Cheadle and the architect was Charles Lynam.
Over the doorway is the MacKenzie crest "Luceo non uro" which means "Enlightenment before law". From the MacKenzie family the House passed to the Church Commissioners who used it as a vicarage to St. Chad's, Freehay until 1927, when Freehay Vicarage was built.
The House then passed back into private ownership.

THE MILL HOUSE, CHEADLE, 1920
The original house on this site is referred to as Mylnehousen and was built in 1542 by the Mylls family. As a result of the marriage of Thomas and Mary Mylls in 1635, the house in the photograph was built and reference was made to it in the marriage settlement of 1638.
It is the second oldest surviving house in Cheadle –
the oldest being Tudor House in High Street which was built in 1558.

CHEADLE.

CHEADLE, c. 1905
This view is from the Mansion House, High Lane and shows the Mansion House gates, now the recreation ground gates. On the opposite side of the road are open fields where the County Primary School and houses built between the World Wars stand today.
The tall spire belongs to the Roman Catholic Church which was designed by A. W. N. Pugin and is considered to be one of his masterpieces. The 200ft.-high spire is a landmark for miles.
The trees in Cheadle Park, on the horizon, were cut down during World War I and used as pit props. High Lane is now called Tean Road.

CHEADLE INFIRMARY, 1968

This was the third workhouse in Cheadle; the previous ones were built in 1735 and 1775.
In 1901 the above Workhouse, later Infirmary, was built by J. Gallimore and designed by J. Snape — both from Newcastle-under-Lyme. The cost of erecting the Infirmary and laundry was £9,749.19s.6d. It was opened on Friday, 20th June, 1902 by the Chairman of the Board of Guardians, Mr. C. J. Blagg.
In 1937, the Guardians handed over administration to the Cheadle Public Assistance Institution and in 1948, they in turn handed over to the National Health Service.

THE EARL OF SHREWSBURY AT CHEADLE, November 2nd, 1946
The Earl of Shrewsbury welcomed in the forecourt of the old Rectory by
Mr. Wilfred Shaw, Secretary of the Cheadle Branch of the British Legion.
The Earl had come to Cheadle to open the Ex-Service Club in Bank Street.

THE ANCIENT ORDER OF FORESTERS, CHEADLE, c. 1920
Members of this Friendly Society are seen here passing the old Cheadle National Boys School on their way to church. In 1931 the old School was sold for £600 to the Diocesan Trust, for use as a Church Hall.
A single storey building was built on the playground, which adjoined the old School, and was named the Carlos Institute.
This was opened in 1939 and was demolished in 1982.

VISIT OF THE LORD BISHOP OF LICHFIELD TO CHEADLE, 10th June, 1939
At 2.35 p.m., the Bishop, Dr. E. S. Woods, consecrated the bells in the Church tower, after a new bell frame had been installed and the bells returned. The contract with Taylors of Loughborough had cost £276. In the photograph, the Bishop is preceded by the Rev. G. R. Thornton, M.A., R.D., Rector of Cheadle 1936-41. Behind the Bishop is the Rev. Hon. Orlando St.Maur Weld-Forrester, M.A., R.D., who had been Rector 1927-36. The Bishop went on to consecrate the extensions of the Carlos Institute.

HIGH STREET, CHEADLE, Pre 1895

This early photograph shows the signs of the many public houses in this small area. On the left is The Angel Inn and on the right, from left to right, are The Wheatsheaf, which is the large white building, Bulls Head, Cross Keys and Royal Oak. Note the wide brick block pavements and the hard core road. The street is busy with deliveries arriving, on the left, and several shoppers on the pavement on the right. The man in the white apron has a large basket, used to deliver bread. Notice the very long striped pole, indicating a barber, above the tobacconist's shop — where a young girl is about to enter.

HIGH STREET, CHEADLE, Pre 1907
From left to right the buildings are: The Angel Inn; Jackson's Iron Warehouse, a general ironmongers with a fascinating display of early farm implements and machinery outside; and the Old Royal Oak, a public house which was closed in 1907 and then converted to a blacksmith's shop, owned by Mr. Sims.

MARKET SQUARE, CHEADLE, 18th September, 1902
The crowds are awaiting the return of Cheadle soldiers, led by
Captain William Shepherd Allen, from the Boer War.
In the foreground is the Cheadle Militia under the command of Mr. Inskip and in the centre are
the Cheadle Town Band and members of the Ancient Order of Foresters, wearing their sashes.
The Parish Office, at the rear, was in use from December 1894 to 1937.
On the steps are members of the Cheadle Parish Council led by the Chairman, Mr. T. B. Cull.

CHEADLE HERALD,
10th August, 1878
Issue No. 49 carried this advertisement for the Hope Inn — a public house without intoxicating drinks!
It closed after about twelve months trading and the furnishings of the Inn were offered for sale by auction on 6th June, 1879.
In opposition to the Hope Inn, at this period, were twenty-five public houses, twelve of which were in High Street.

AUGUST 10, 1878. SATURDAY,

HOPE INN!

Public House without Intoxicating Drinks!
HIGH STREET, CHEADLE.

PRIVATE ROOM FOR LADIES.

TARIFF—

	BAR.	SITTING ROOM.	BEST ROOM.
Tea, per cup	1d.	1½d.	2d.
Coffee	,,	,,	,,
Cocoa	,,	,,	,,
New Milk, per glass	,,	,,	,,
Ginger Beer	,,	,,	,,
Lemonade	2d.	2½d.	3d.
Soda Water	,,	,,	,,
Liquors	,,	,,	,,
Man's Best Friend	½d.	1d.	1½d.
Buns	,,	,,	,,
	1d.	1½d.	2d.
,, buttered	1½d.	2d.	2½d.
Scones	1d.	1½d.	2d.
,, buttered	1½d.	2d.	2½d.
Sandwiches	2d.	2½d.	3d.
Plate of Ham	4d.	4½d.	5d.
Plate of Beef	,,	,,	,,
Meat Pies	2d.	2½d.	3d.
Bread and Cheese	2d.	,,	,,
Plain Tea	6d.	7d.	8d.
,, with Eggs	8d.	9d.	10d.
,, with Ham	10d.	11d.	1s.
,, with Chop or Steak	10d.	1s.	1s. 1d.
Cheese only	1d.	1½d.	2d.
A Wash, clean Towel	,,	,,	,,

CONFECTIONERY.

Billiards, Chess, Draughts, Smoke Room, Newspapers, Tobacco, Cigars, &c.

GAMBLING AND SWEARING PROHIBITED.

Visitors to Town, or Alton, bringing their own food supplied with hot water and attendance for 2d. each.

ALL ARE WELCOME!

Open from 6.30 a.m. to 10 p.m.

HIGH STREET, CHEADLE,
1931
Telephone poles were erected in Cheadle in 1904 and, because so few people had telephones, the wires went over the roof tops from street to street.
For example:
High Street to Back Street and Charles Street to Chapel Street.
In 1931 the new automatic telephone exchange was opened in Mill Road and normal street wiring was installed.
Here the workmen are removing the old "over the roof tops" wires and have placed a flag in the road to warn oncoming motorists.
On the opposite side of the street is The Unicorn public house.

FIRST AID AND AIR RAID PRECAUTIONS VOLUNTEERS, CHEADLE, 1940
The photograph was taken in the forecourt of the Guildhall in Tape Street and shows the first volunteers to enrol in Cheadle's First Aid and Air Raid Precautions Services. Doctor George Saint was in charge of the First Aid Group and Mr. Plato Joseph Breed was in charge of the Air Raid Precautions Unit.
Some of the A. R. P. wardens are wearing their protective helmets.

61

CHEADLE
:: RURAL DISTRICT COUNCIL ::

OPENING OF

NEW COUNCIL CHAMBER
AND OFFICES

At Leek Road, Cheadle
On FRIDAY, MARCH 5th, 1937, at 3 p.m.

BY

D. HEATH, Esq., J.P.

CHEADLE R. D. C. OFFICES,
1937

The picture shows the cover of the programme for the opening of the Cheadle Rural District Council Offices on 5th March, 1937. The design of the Offices was by regulations set by the Royal Institute of British Architects, in open competition and sealed award. Contract price was to be between £6,500 and £8,500.

Over twenty designs were received and it was awarded to the architects W. J. Venables and C. F. Barker of Hanley. The tender to build the offices was accepted by Tompkinson and Betteley of Longton, at the contract price of £7,792.

The heating and ventilation contract awarded to T. S. Hedley, costing £282, and electrical installation by F. W. Langley, costing £218.

The building was opened by the Council Chairman, D. Heath, Esq., J.P.

In the vestibule, a short service was followed by the unveiling of a tablet by the oldest Councillor. After refreshments in the Chamber, there was a tour of the Offices.

CHEADLE R. D. C. OFFICES, 1939
Workmen are filling sandbags at the rear of the Council Offices after the outbreak of War in 1939.
The sandbags are covering the Foundation Stone laid on 27th March, 1936 by the then Chairman of the Cheadle R. D. C., Councillor William Podmore.

THE WAR MEMORIAL, CHEADLE, 29th May, 1949
This is the ceremony of Dedication and Unveiling of the War Memorial Gardens,
in the recreation ground. The Master of Ceremonies was Mr. W. R. Raine.
Dr. Coullie formally opened the Gardens, Rev. Russell Shearer gave an address and the
Dedication Service was conducted by the Rector, Rev. Alfred Jones.
A member of the organising committee was Mr. W. Maclean who represented the British Legion.
Mrs. Robina Berry represented the Women's Section of the British Legion.

TAPE STREET, CHEADLE, December 1947
This photograph was taken to show the Christmas display at William Alcock's butcher's shop. From left to right are: William Alcock; his daughter Kathleen; his brother Harry Alcock and Dy Davies, licensee of the Station Hotel, next door.

CHAPEL LANE, KINGSLEY HOLT, c. 1930
The old Primitive Methodist Chapel was built in 1870 and used until the new Chapel was erected in 1937.
It was then sold, for £32, to Mr. Chester who used it as a chicken breeding centre, a business continued by his son-in-law, Mr. W. Sutcliffe.
The building was demolished when Mr. Sutcliffe retired.

METHODIST CHAPEL, KINGSLEY HOLT, 24th July, 1937
The photograph shows Mr. Stephen W. Goodwin laying one of the Foundation Stones of the new Chapel, watched by Rev. Henshall.
The builders were Messrs. J. Hurst & Son of Cheadle and the building cost £1,500.
The architects were Messrs. Pennington, Hustler and Taylor of Pontefract.
The Chapel was planned to seat eighty adults with Sunday School accommodation for one hundred children.

SIDNEY DRIVE, KINGSLEY HOLT, 1921
Cutting the first sods on the site of the new Council Houses, is Sidney Goodwin,
on the left, who was doing so on behalf of Cheadle Rural District Council.
The architects were Watts and Twemlow and the sixty houses were built by J. W. Kent of Burslem.
The cost to the Council was for thirty of Type "A" at £865 each; twenty-four of Type "B" at £965 each;
six of Type "B4" at £1,015 each and £2,348 for roads and drains.
The houses were to be rented out at a weekly rate of: 10/- for Type "A"; 12/- for "B" and 14/- for "B4".
Preference was given to prospective tenants if they had served in H.M. Forces.

THE SHAWE, KINGSLEY, 1919

This was the former home of the Lords of the Manor of Kingsley — the Stubbs and Beech families. The House was rebuilt in 1821 and sold as Lot 16 in the auction of the Beech estates on 25th September, 1919.

At the time of the sale it was described as "An attractive country residence with garden and pleasure grounds, farm and outbuildings, fish ponds, cottage and woodlands with 264 acres of land. The Shawe, after falling into decay over many years, was finally demolished in 1987.

KINGSLEY RECTORY, c. 1908
This is the third Rectory of Kingsley. Built in 1822, it replaced an earlier Rectory
which is still in being in Hazel Cross Road.
In 1956, the building was sold to Mr. J. Taylor and
a new Rectory was built on an adjoining site in Glebe Road.

KINGSLEY, c. 1910

On the left, in the background, is Kingsley Endowed School. It was built in 1818 out of the funds of the John Stubbs Charity — which is still in existence. A piece of land was purchased for £130 and the school and house were erected thereon, at a cost of £412.12s.6d. The 55,000 bricks used to build the School were bought by the Trustees, at cost price, from the Duke of Devonshire's brick works nearby.
On the right is the Plough Inn with a horse and cart from Bunting's Brewery, Uttoxeter.

KINGSLEY JUNIOR SCHOOL, 1933
The photograph shows Class 6 with their teacher, Mr. H. A. Chester.
The Headmaster at the time was Mr. W. C. Mansell.
Other teachers were Mr. E. Critchlow, Mrs. K. Shufflebotham, Miss Adams,
Miss Morris, Mrs. Hall and Miss Jackson.

ST. WERBURGH'S CHURCH, KINGSLEY, c. 1904

The original Church was consecrated in 1221. On 26th August, 1817, a decision was made to rebuild the church. The contract was awarded to Thomas Trubshaw of Great Haywood and on 6th July, 1819, when the first stone of the new Church was laid, his expenses were two shillings. The Church was opened later that year, the costs being shared by Kingsley and Whiston parishes. Kingsley's share was £1,316.3s.3½d., being three fifths of the total, and Whiston's share £870.12s.8d. The chancel and vestry were rebuilt and a new porch added in 1886. The chancel was consecrated and reopened on 4th September, 1886.

ST. WERBURGH'S CHURCH, KINGSLEY, Pre 1886
An old print of the interior of the Church, prior to alterations in 1886;
showing box pews, lamps, a flat ceiling and a small chancel.

ST. WERBURGH'S CHURCH, KINGSLEY, c. 1910
The interior of the Church looks very different after the alterations of 1886.
The five lights of the East Window are in memory of Joseph Alcock. The pulpit, on the left, is in memory of John and Jane Docksey and dates from 1890 — the old pulpit having been transferred to Whiston Church. The organ, by Jardine of Manchester, was installed in 1909. The removal of the old organ and installation of the new one cost £225. Also in the chancel are the Sanctus Bell, Bishop's chair, reading desk, lectern and reading table — all given in memory of loved ones.
Kingsley Church, as at Forsbrook and Caverswall, is a "weeping church".

HIGH STREET, KINGSLEY, 1910

On the left, Mr. Sutton, the postmaster, is standing outside the village Post Office.
On the far right, sideways on to the street, is a house known as Canada House with, next door, the Temperance Hall. Both were built for Miss Shepherd. The Hall dates from 1858 and is now the Victory Café.
Beyond is the "old smithy" which bears a date of 1762.
In the right foreground are the railings of the Wesleyan Chapel, first registered on 22nd January, 1812.
During World War II the Chapel was used by Kingsley Home Guard and in 1947 it was closed for worship.
The building is now a 'bus garage.

PRIMITIVE METHODIST CHAPEL, KINGSLEY, 1911

A fustian mill, operated by J. & N. Philips & Co. of Tean, stood on this site from 1790 — 1822. The mill was converted to a chapel, to be replaced by this Chapel in 1910. The photograph shows, from left to right: Mr. William Hood; Mr. Herbert Hood; Mrs. Ann Cooper and Mr. Joseph Hood who was the organist and caretaker. The last service was held on 28th April, 1985 and the Chapel closed.

THE WINDMILL, WERRINGTON, c. 1906
Built in the eighteenth century the Mill had four sails, but it ceased to be wind-driven at the end of the nineteenth century.
From 1850 — 1870, Mark Greatbatch was the miller. William Forister was then miller until 1880, when he took over the public house — The Windmill.
The Werrington Home Guard used the windmill as its headquarters from 1940-45 and in 1952, the Midlands Electricity Board took over the site.

NEW WORKS FOR THE MANUFACTURE OF BLADING FOR STEAM TURBINES.
THOMAS BOLTON & SONS, LTD., 1911.

THOMAS BOLTON & SONS' WORKS, FROGHALL, 1911
The first works at Froghall were opened in 1890.
In 1961, Boltons became part of the B. I. C. C. Group and then in April 1984, Boltons merged with Johnson & Nephew (Non-Ferrous) Ltd. to form
Thomas Bolton and Johnson Ltd.
On the right of the picture are the Froghall lime kilns which operated from 1777 to 1942. This is now a conservation area.

THOMAS BOLTON & SONS LTD., FROGHALL, 1910
Part of the interior of Thomas Bolton's copper works at Froghall showing men pouring molten copper into ingots.
The men are all wearing strong protective gloves on their right hands so that they could grip the hot handles of the ladles.

THE WOODHOUSE, LOCKWOOD ROAD, CHEADLE, 1908
First evidence of this house appears in a bill of sale dated 29th September, 1820.
In 1845 Mr. John Bill, the owner, was allocated Pew No. 1 in the South Gallery of
Cheadle Church — to seat ten people. Mr. Cecil Wedgwood, who was the first Lord Mayor
of the City of Stoke-on-Trent, was resident here in 1906. His family continued to live here until 1939,
when it was registered by the Air Ministry. After the war it was returned to the Wedgwood family
who retained it until 1985, when it was sold to the Cheadle Methodist Church.

JOHN MASEFIELD, POET LAUREATE AT THE OFFICIAL OPENING OF THE MASEFIELD MEMORIAL GATEWAY, HAWKSMOOR, OCT 21, 1933.

HAWKSMOOR NATURE RESERVE, 21st October, 1933
The Reserve originally covered an area of 200 acres. It was bought by public subscription, organised by Mr. J. R. B. Masefield. It was presented to the National Trust on 7th May, 1927 and the opening ceremony was performed by Lord Grey of Falloden. When Mr. Masefield died in 1932, the main gates were built at the Reserve to honour the Founder's memory and they were opened by his cousin, the then Poet Laureate, John Masefield on 21st October, 1933. Since that time, further woods and moorland have been given or bought and the Reserve now extends to over 300 acres.

GREENDALE COTTAGES, 1910
This attractive terrace was built in 1839 as eight cottages for the workmen at
Thomas Patten's copper and brass works at Oakamoor.
In 1964 they were purchased by Mrs. Aldridge, a retired Stoke-on-Trent headmistress.
Mrs. Aldridge had the cottages modernised and converted the eight cottages to five and lived
in one of them. On her death in March 1986, she left the Greendale Cottages, together with
an adjoining field and five acres of woodland, rich in wildlife, to the National Trust.

LIGHTOAKS, OAKAMOOR, c. 1912
Colonel Wilson Patten had this house built upon the remains of old farm buildings in the 1820's. The Colonel, who was Member of Parliament for South Lancashire, married a Miss Hyde of Wootton Lodge and when he was later elevated to the peerage he took the name Lord Winnaleigh. The house was sold by auction in 1872 and purchased by Alfred Sohier Bolton, whose family retained it into the 1980's.

PARISH CHURCH, OAKAMOOR.

HOLY TRINITY CHURCH, OAKAMOOR, c. 1906

In 1831 the Patten family donated £100, sufficient land and stone for the building of the Church. The National Society agreed to contribute £70 towards the extra cost of £100, providing that a school and church were built at the same time. To a design by Trubshaw of Great Haywood, the two school rooms — 30ft. by 14ft. — sufficient for 70 boys and 70 girls were built on the ground floor and the Church was built above. The Church was consecrated by Bishop Ryder on 18th August, 1832 and Oakamoor became an ecclesiastical parish in 1864. The school closed in 1856 and is now used as a parish room.

OAKAMOOR, c. 1890

At the rear is the Church with the National School, 1856-71, to the left of it. This school was demolished in 1944, the stone being used for the building of a wall around the Churchyard extension. In the centre of the picture, down Mill Road, is a group of terraced houses, one of which has a sign board in front — this was the "Admiral Jervis" from 1832 to 1871. Further down Mill Road, on the left of the picture, is the building where Alfred Bolton started his own school in 1871. This was "for his workers' children" and was to remain open until he built the present school in 1891. In the foreground is Bolton's Brass and Copper Company, situated here from 1852 to 1963. The site is now a picnic area.

MILL ROAD, OAKAMOOR, c. 1905
An interesting group of people pose for the photographer outside the village Post Office. From the left we can see Clement Tipper and his son Clement; Frank Kerry on the horse; and Ensor Titterton with the mail cart, which was brought from Cheadle.
Oakamoor had three mail bags delivered from Cheadle. One was delivered to this Post Office for local delivery, one went to the copper works and the other to the Bolton family.

OAKAMOOR RAILWAY STATION, c. 1910
This photograph was taken from the top of the tunnel and shows the station with a train en route from Leek to Uttoxeter. The station was situated on the Churnet Valley line and opened in 1849.
The houses on the left were built by the railway authorities for rail workers and called The Island.
In the foreground is the Gate House — at the level crossing.
The line was closed on 4th January, 1965 and the station was demolished.
The track was taken up and the area is now under conservation.

OAKAMOOR BRIDGE, c. 1906

The condition of the old wooden bridge over the Churnet, at a place called Oakamore, was reported to the Quarter Sessions at Easter 1708. At the next Court Sessions it was agreed to build a stone cart bridge to carry 300 tons weight of stone. The bridge was built in 1709-10 with the Court paying instalments or benevolents as follows: 1708 — £100; 1709 — £80; 1710 — £50 and 1712 — £8. The bridge was widened in 1778 to comply with the turnpike requirements and that same bridge is still retained by the Staffordshire County Council.

OAKAMOOR, c. 1905
The Cricketers Arms is on the immediate left.
The earth roadway leads into the village and on the right-hand side,
behind the group of ladies in their long white aprons, is the Village Hall.
On the roadside, immediately behind the Hall, is the Methodist Chapel and to the left
of the Chapel the white building is the Lord Nelson public house.

OAKAMOOR, c. 1905

This view of the village is from the lime kilns and shows, in the bottom left hand corner, the Cricketers Arms public house with the Toll House to the right.

In the distance, amongst the trees, is Oakamoor Memorial Church, with the spire of Oakamoor Mills School showing to the left. This School was donated and opened by Mr. A. S. Bolton on 1st February, 1892. Its upkeep was maintained and administered by the Bolton family until 4th May, 1953, when it was taken over by the Staffordshire County Council Education Committee.

THE MEMORIAL FREE CHURCH, OAKAMOOR, c. 1920
The Church was erected in 1876 by Alfred Sohier Bolton, replacing an earlier building which he had converted to a chapel in 1868. The architect was Edward F. C. Clarke of London and the East Window was designed by James Powell and Sons of Whitefriars, London. The Church was opened on Easter Sunday, 21st April, 1878 and the first Chaplain was Rev. Charles Denman. A vestry was added in 1931.
The Bolton family are still patrons and the present minister is Rev. Leonard Fountain, M.A.

THE LODGE, OAKAMOOR, c. 1920

The Lodge was built in the late eighteenth century. Residents include the Wragge family, one of whom, George Wragge, jnr., was a partner at the copper works.

In 1828, he received £200 per annum plus free rent of Oakamoor Lodge.

The Lodge was purchased by Colonel Wilson Patten of Lightoaks in 1872 and three years later he sold it to Mr. Thomas Bolton who moved in with his family in 1880. Mr. Bolton lived there until 1902, when his niece Sarah and her husband, Dr. P. Bearblock moved in. They resided there until their deaths in 1948 and 1951 respectively. Soon afterwards the Lodge was demolished.

"JIMMY'S YARD", OAKAMOOR, 1900
The scene shows a visiting preacher using a North Staffordshire Railway truck as a platform to address an open air congregation. The white painted building on the left is the Lord Nelson Inn. In 1913, the first telephone was used in the village — the call being made from the copper works to the Lord Nelson Inn. On the right, the first house facing the camera was used as a doctor's surgery. The doctor came from Alton, daily at first and then three times a week. Doctor Chalmers began the surgery, to be followed by Dr. Webster. The surgery closed in the 1960's.

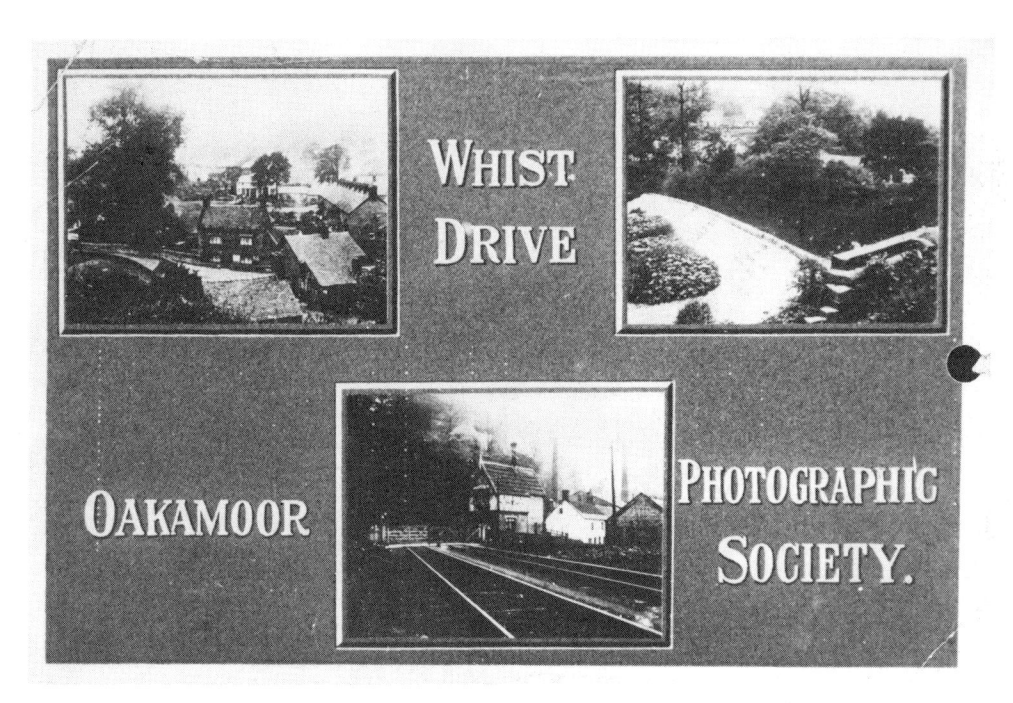

OAKAMOOR PHOTOGRAPHIC SOCIETY, c. 1910
These photographs are on the reverse side of a Whist Drive score card.
The pictures are: on the left — a view of Oakamoor; on the right — the Weir;
at the bottom — the railway Gate House and crossing gates.

"E Tenebris Oritur Lux."

The Oakamoor Electric Lighting Committee beg to call your attention to and to ask your assistance for the Bazaar, Jumble Sale and Open Air Fete, which they intend holding on August 5th, 1907. The proceeds to be devoted to paying off the debt on the Lighting Scheme.

The Electric Light has been recently installed for outside lighting throughout the Village by voluntary effort, and this has entailed an expenditure of about £200.

The inhabitants of the Village are making every effort to clear off the debt, and in order to do this the more speedily they are appealing to their friends for assistance.

Gifts of money, fancy goods, new or left-off wearing apparel or anything saleable, will be gratefully accepted.

OAKAMOOR ELECTRIC LIGHTING COMMITTEE,
1907
"E Tenebris Oritur Lux"
(Out of darkness comes light)
Electric lighting, at 100 volts, was first switched on in the Oakamoor works by Sir George Robertson in 1887 and was installed in the village by December 1906. The Mill School classrooms already had electricity, as evidenced by two quotes from the log book.
On 18th December, 1896, it states:
"I believe the electric lamps are to be overhauled" and according to the entry for 19th November, 1900, Oakamoor evening classes could not be held "owing to the failure in the electric light".

DEMOLITION OF MILL CHIMNEY, OAKAMOOR,
11th September, 1963
When the site was cleared of all the Bolton's Mill works buildings, it was handed over to Staffordshire County Council to be designated as a leisure and conservation area.
The bell from the old rolling mill was given by Bolton's to St. Mildred's Church, Whiston.

Oakamoor Mill Chimney

Demolished on Sept. 11th 1963 at 3.54 pm. Height of Chimney 145 ft (approx) Wt. of Chimney 750 Tons (approx) Time taken to fall 7 seconds.

97

OAKAMOOR BOWLING CLUB, 1943
The Club played on the Bolton's sports ground.
The photograph depicts the Oakamoor Club team, captained by Colin Cope —
standing in the centre wearing a waistcoat — and a local R. A. F. team,
captained by George Aldridge — standing to the left of Mr. Cope.

MOOR COURT, OAKAMOOR, 1920

In 1860, Alfred S. Bolton purchased a house and had it extended. He called it Moor Court. The architect for the extension was William Sugden of Leek.

In March 1862, the Bolton family moved in and they retained the house until 1955, when it was sold to the Home Office for use as a Women's Correction Centre.

In 1983, Moor Court and the surrounding buildings on the estate were offered for sale and passed back into private hands.

MOTOR RACE, COTTON, Pre 1904
The finish line of an early motor race meeting at the Star Inn crossroads at Cotton.
Note that the car does not have a registration number — thus dating the photograph as pre-1904.
Car registration became compulsory on 1st January, 1904.

ST. WILFRED'S ELEMENTARY SCHOOL, COTTON, 23rd August, 1897
The School was built at the expense of the Countess of Shrewsbury in 1848 and the Earl endowed it with £65 per annum, from 1852-57. The School was conducted by Passionists and upon their departure it became a dame school, conducted by Miss Goldsworthy. Owing to lack of pupils the School closed in the 1860's but in 1873 it was used as a dormitory for the senior boys of Cotton College. In 1875, the building was used as a dwelling house and in 1897, when the house became vacant, Father Buscot reopened the Roman Catholic School. The first teacher was Miss Alice Powell who received a salary of £52 per annum. After reorganisation in 1948, it became a Roman Catholic Primary School and was later renamed the Father Faber School.

ST. JOHN'S CHURCH, COTTON, 1960

This little Church was erected as a Chapel of Ease in 1795 and consecrated on 4th July, 1795. It was built by Thomas Gilbert who was Squire of Cotton and owned Cotton Hall. He was Member of Parliament for Newcastle-under-Lyme from 1763-68 and was then, for twenty seven years, Member for Lichfield. He died at Cotton on 18th December, 1798 and two days later was buried beneath his Chapel.
By order of Council dated 21st July, 1932, the Benefice of Cotton was united with that of Oakamoor so that Cotton and Oakamoor shared one vicar.

St. Wilfrid's College, Cotton

COTTON HALL AND ST. WILFRED'S COLLEGE, c. 1908
Title Deeds of the Hall go back to 1601 and, for over 150 years, it was the home of the Gilbert family. In 1843 it was sold to the 16th Earl of Shrewsbury, being intended as a home for his nephew, Bertram. In 1846 the Earl gave it to Father Faber and his Brothers of the Will of God. They had St. Wilfred's Church built at a cost of £2,500. It was designed by Pugin and is on the right of the picture — with the spire. It was consecrated on 25th April, 1848.
The Hall was taken over by the Sedgeley Park Preparatory School in 1868 and extensions were added in 1874, 1886 and 1931. The School closed in July 1987.

THE ROMAN CATHOLIC PRIEST'S HOUSE, ALTON, 1930
This building is listed on the 1843 Tithe Award.
In July 1855 Dr. Winter, who was Parish Priest at Alton, asked for some Sisters from the Carlow Convent of Mercy in Ireland to take charge of his schools and "these were installed in a little convent near to the Church".
This convent is now the Priest's House.

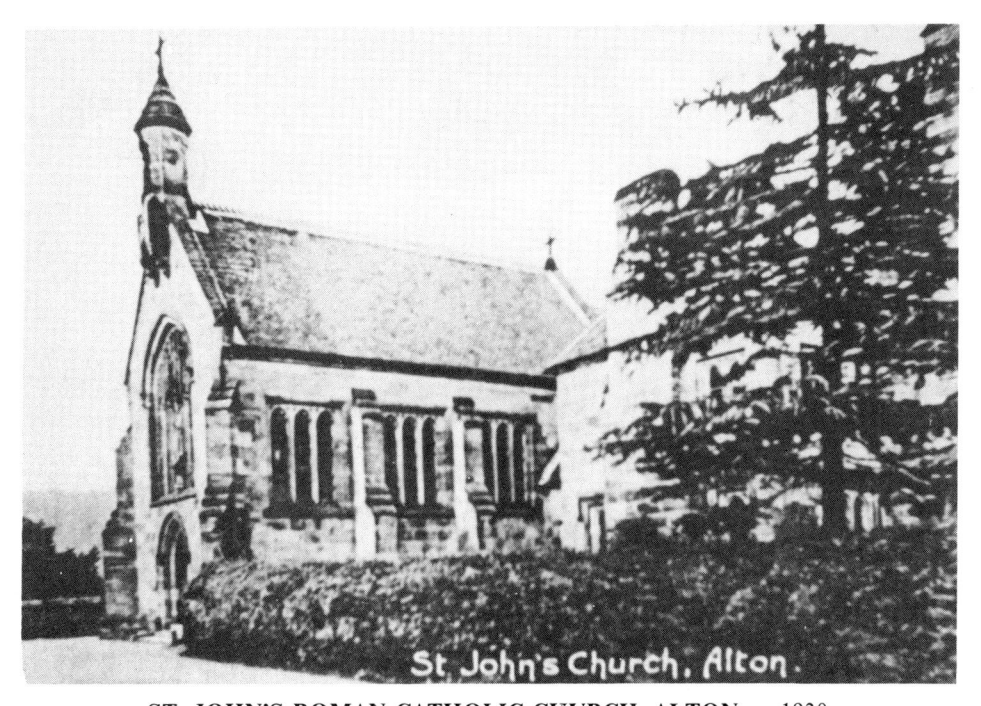

ST. JOHN'S ROMAN CATHOLIC CHURCH, ALTON, c. 1930
The Church was designed and built by Augustus W. Pugin and dedicated by
Bishop Walsh on 13th July, 1842.
On the left-hand side of the Altar, which was sculpted by Thomas Roddis,
is the resting place of the 16th Earl and Countess of Shrewsbury.
The resting place of the 17th Earl is on the right-hand side of the Altar.

ALTON CASTLE, c. 1912
A castle was erected on this site during Saxon times. It was replaced by another erected in the twelfth century by Bertram de Verdun.
The ruins of his castle were augmented into the present castle when it was built by A. W. Pugin during the years 1840-42.
The Castle was purchased by the Congregation of the Sisters of Mercy in 1919 and is used as a Preparatory School for boys and girls aged between 3 and 13.
In the bottom foreground is The Old Mill which was used for over 100 years as a flint mill and later as a saw mill.
It closed in 1944.

ST. PETER'S CHURCH OF ENGLAND CHURCH, ALTON, c. 1910

The Church was originally consecrated on 1st June, 1267 by Eyon, Bishop of St. Asaph. It was partially rebuilt in 1830 with a new roof, south wall, resetting of old windows and tower repairs costing £932.18s.0d. Further rebuilding took place in 1885, when it had a new oak roof, choir stalls, floor tiles and an enlarged Altar. It was reopened by the Bishop of the Diocese on 11th April, 1885. In 1935 the plaster was stripped from the north wall and the fresco depicting the "Garden of Eden" was found. Electricity was installed in the Church in 1936 and in 1952 the old Altar was replaced by one from St. Oswald's, Ashbourne. The building to the right was the Police Station, erected by the 16th Earl of Shrewsbury in 1849. It is now a private residence.

THE ROUND HOUSE, ALTON, c. 1925
Erected in 1815, this was used as a lock-up or house of correction.
In the far left of the picture, behind the tree, was the Old Iron Room.
The detached house in the centre of the street was a blacksmith's shop, operated by a Mr. Smith from Rocester, before being demolished in 1926-27. On the right of the picture, the house with a bay window and railings has been the Post Office since 1909, except for about ten years from 1930-40, when it was housed in Cedar Hill. In the right foreground is Warners' drapery.

HIGH STREET, ALTON, c. 1915
On the left is The Staffordshire Knot public house which was closed in 1967, the last licensee being Mr. Wetwood. The stone house, in the centre, was formerly The Castle Inn, which closed in 1914. Further along the left-hand side of the street is Llewelyn's sweet shop, with a lady in the doorway. Next door is Jenkin's shop. On the right-hand side is The Bull's Head and next door Mr. Aked Byatt's shop, selling roller blinds and clothing and which later became the Co-op.

ALTON NATIONAL SCHOOL
Erected in 1845, it replaced a building which was used as the Anthony Wall Charity School, endowed and opened in 1721. The School was extended on land given by Rev. Pike Jones whose family crest — three rooks — can be seen on the central exterior wall. The architect was Mr. T. Fradgley of Uttoxeter and it cost £300 of which the National Society gave £160 and the Government gave £108.
The School closed in 1893 when a new school was built at Town Head. The old building was bought by Mr. Byatt, a grocer, for £100 and in 1987 the building was sold as a private residence.

THE CHURCH ARMY VAN AT ALTON, 1923
This was the No. 1 van "Lichfield" which was manned by Sister Meredith and
Sister Clarke, on their visit to Town Head, Alton.
They normally stayed for a period of a few days, holding services in the area.

COMIC CARD FROM ALTON, c. 1908
Many cards of this type were published in the early years of the twentieth century. The place names were added according to the orders received by the publishers.

112

ALTON STATION, DURING THE FLOOD, 26th/27th July, 1927
The railway was cut through the Churnet Valley in 1847 by George Stevenson.
The line through Alton was constructed at the expense of the 16th Earl of Shrewsbury
and opened at midday on 30th April, 1849. The station building was designed by Pugin.
In 1851, ten trains ran daily, five to Uttoxeter and five to Leek. On Tuesdays and
Thursdays there was a connecting 'bus to Alton Towers.
The railway closed in January 1965 and the station is now owned by the Landmark Trust.

ALVETON LODGE, 1807

It is recorded in 1339 as "a certain plot called the Lodge with a certain ruinous dove cote and 480 acres of poor marsh uncultivated land, value 12d".
In 1807 the 15th Earl of Shrewsbury began converting the Lodge into Alton Abbey and engaged J. C. Louden to lay out the gardens, walks, woods, out buildings, conservatories, etc. This sketch shows the East Front of the Lodge before any conversion work had taken place.

ALTON ABBEY, 1830

The accounts for building the Abbey start in 1809 and end in 1813 and state that —
Mr. Fower received the sum of £581.14s.5½d. for building part of the South Front of the Abbey;
Mr. Baily received £721.13s.1d. for building part of Abbey House and altering stables;
Mr. Plant, plumber and glazier, received £406.9s.2d; Josiah Wedgwood received £4.2s.0d.
for plaster and the Duke of Devonshire received £25 for a black marble square.
In 1811-12 a garden and pleasure ground were developed at a total cost of £2,588.

ALTON TOWERS, 1920
In the centre is the stained glass window of the Banquet Hall, designed by Pugin in 1848, and to the left is the gothic tower of the Chapel.
In 1924 the Earl of Shrewsbury sold the estate and it was purchased by a private company who began to develop the site as a conservation and leisure park area.

THE BANQUET HALL, ALTON TOWERS, c. 1929
After the sale of the estate in 1924, the Hall was the venue for afternoon teas and social functions.
During World War II the building was used by the Army as 163 Officer Cadet Training Unit and Tower Hamlet Rifles.
In 1948, the Towers caught fire destroying the wooden panelling seen in the picture.

**THE CHAPEL,
ALTON TOWERS,** c. 1930
The Chapel was built by the 16th Earl of Shrewsbury in 1830 and was registered for Roman Catholics at the Michaelmas Session of that year by the Earl and his priest, Dr. Daniel Rock.
On the sale of the estate in 1924, the Altar was sold for 30 shillings and the brass Altar Cross, with ruby glass mounts and standing 41 inches high, was sold for two guineas.

THE FLAG TOWER, ALTON TOWERS, c. 1910 Built around 1810 to 1813, the Tower was designed by Mr. Ireland and the stone mason was Henry Fower. Over the four years it took to build the Tower, the accounts show that £806.12s.9d. was spent by various contractors, including on 6th October, 1810, £4.4s.0d. spent on "ale at the laying of the foundation of the Tower".

THE EARL'S DRIVE, ALTON, c. 1920
Dimmingsdale Lodge stands midway along the Oakamoor to Alton Road.
It was built by Charles, 15th Earl of Shrewsbury in 1810 at the time of the construction
of the roadways and drives in the area.
In 1979 it was a derelict property with no water, electricity, sanitation or other services.
After much renovation by the proprietor, Mrs. M. A. Keeling, it opened in 1981
as the Ramblers Retreat Restaurant.